David Beckham

By Jeff Savage

AMAZING
ATHLETES

Lerner Publications Company • Minneapolis

For Taylor and Bailey—always remember to hustle, be aggressive, and S.I.U.!

Lerner Publications Company
A division of Lerner Publishing Group, Inc.
241 First Avenue North
Minneapolis, MN 55401 U.S.A.

Website address: www.lernerbooks.com

Library of Congress Cataloging-in-Publication Data

Savage, Jeff, 1961–
    David Beckham / by Jeff Savage.
      p.   cm. — (Amazing athletes)
    Includes index.
    ISBN 978-0-8225-8834-4 (lib. bdg. : alk. paper)
    1. Beckham, David, 1975—-Juvenile literature. 2. Soccer players—England—Biography—Juvenile literature. I. Title.
    GV942.7.B432S28 2008
    796.334092—dc22 [B]   2007035032

Manufactured in the United States of America
2 3 4 5 6 7 – BP – 13 12 11 10 09 08

TABLE OF CONTENTS

Cameras swarm in front of David *(on bench, third from right)* before his first game with the Los Angeles Galaxy.

JOINING OUR GALAXY

David Beckham was surrounded. Nearly 100 photographers were taking pictures of him in his Los Angeles Galaxy uniform. Behind him, more than 27,000 fans had packed the Home Depot Center near Los Angeles, California. Many Hollywood movie stars were in the crowd.

All of these people had come to see David's first game in the United States' top soccer league, MLS (Major League Soccer). The crowd had a good reason to be excited. David Beckham is the most famous soccer player in the world. In fact, David might be the most famous athlete in the world.

David wears the number 23 for the LA Galaxy. He said he chose the number to honor basketball legend Michael Jordan, who also wore 23.

U.S. soccer fans had high hopes for David. They hoped that his dazzling style of play would make soccer as popular with Americans as football, basketball, and baseball.

There was just one problem, though. David was injured. So when the game started, David was sitting on the bench. Everyone in the stadium hoped he would get a chance to play.

David had gained fame with his perfect **crossing passes** from anywhere on the field. But he was best known for his **free kicks**. David could boom the ball nearly 100 miles per hour (160 kilometers per hour). Better yet, he had a gift for making his kicks bend around a wall of opponents.

As the game went on, the excitement kept building. Then, with 12 minutes left in the game, David took the

The crowd goes wild as David *(right)* checks into the game.

David steps into a **corner kick**.

field. The crowd roared, and camera flashes lit up the stadium.

The Galaxy were trailing, 1–0. On one of his first **possessions**, David kicked the ball 60 yards (55 meters) downfield. The beautiful pass sailed directly to teammate Quavas Kirk. The crowd roared, but the Galaxy failed to score.

Moments later, David got the ball again. He dribbled forward but was cut down by a sliding defender. The Galaxy superstar landed hard on the grass. The crowd groaned as David rolled around in pain. After a moment, David staggered to his feet and played on. The game ended soon after. The Galaxy lost by a goal, but hardly anyone cared. They had seen soccer history. "The reaction to me was incredible," David told reporters afterward. "This has truly been the most remarkable week of my life."

David salutes the crowd at the end of the match.

David's parents, Ted and Sandra Beckham, are both soccer fans.

MAKING GOALS

David Robert Joseph Beckham was born May 2, 1975, in London, England. He grew up in the nearby town of Chingford. His father, David "Ted" Beckham, worked as a plumber. His mother, Sandra, was a hairdresser. David has two sisters, Lynne and Joanne.

David was a shy, well-behaved boy. His favorite subject in elementary school was art. He also enjoyed sports, such as basketball, rugby, and long-distance running. His favorite sport was soccer, which is called football in Europe.

The Beckhams were big fans of the popular Manchester United Football Club. They often traveled together to see the team play. Like millions of other British boys, David dreamed of playing for the great Man U team.

Manchester United is one of the most famous sports teams in the world. The team has more than 50 million fans and 200 official fan clubs.

When he was eight years old, David joined a local youth soccer team. His coach and his father helped him learn the arts

The Man U team (shown here in a 1982 game) are called the Red Devils for their red shirts.

of dribbling, passing, and shooting. David developed excellent footwork and a gift for keeping the ball away from **defenders**.

David was 11 years old when he came off the field one day after a game. "It's good that you played well today," his mother told him, "because Manchester United were watching you, and they want you to come down and have a trial." David looked up at his mother with wide eyes. He began crying with joy.

The trial was a soccer skills tournament. The most talented boys in England showed off their skills to a panel of judges. David won the event with the highest score ever! His reward was a trip to a soccer camp.

Over the next few years, David continued to improve his game. Pro teams kept an eye on his progress. Then, on July 8, 1991, David's dream came true. Manchester United offered him a **contract**. At just 16 years old, he joined the club as a **trainee**.

Manchester U's youth team *(above)* parades with their 1992 Football Association Youth Cup trophy at the 1993 finals.

STARDOM

David spent the next few years developing his skills on Man U's youth team. Near the end of the 1994–1995 season, David was called up to the **English Premier League (EPL)** team. He was just 19 years old, but he had reached the top level of his sport.

The following season, David was named a starting **midfielder**. This meant he needed to cover both ends of the field. The position was a good match for David's cross-country running experience. He ran tirelessly up and down the field. After Man U lost its first game, the team won its next five matches. Man U surprised the soccer world by going on to win the Premier League title and the FA Cup.

In the first game of the 1996–1997 season, David gained fame on an amazing play. Toward the end of a match against Wimbledon, David took the ball at midfield. He noticed Wimbledon goalkeeper Neil Sullivan was standing far out from the net. David drilled a high, booming kick from 60 yards (55 m) away. The ball sailed over everyone and curled into the net for a goal!

David celebrates his incredible goal against Wimbledon. Man U went on to win the game 3–0.

David's spectacular play made the front page of British newspapers. It was the talk of the soccer world. The victory started Man U on a 15-game unbeaten streak. The team won its second league title in a row. David was voted the Premiership's Young Player of the Year.

The following spring, David saw a music video of the popular musical group the Spice Girls. One of the girls, "Posh Spice," caught his eye. Her real name was Victoria Adams, and the two soon met in person. They began dating.

Victoria Adams and David Beckham

On the field, David enjoyed a huge 1997–1998 season. He scored a career-best 9 goals for Man U. After matches, he signed autographs for fans and posed for photographers. Companies such as Gillette, Adidas, and Coca-Cola paid him millions to promote their products. He was a superstar.

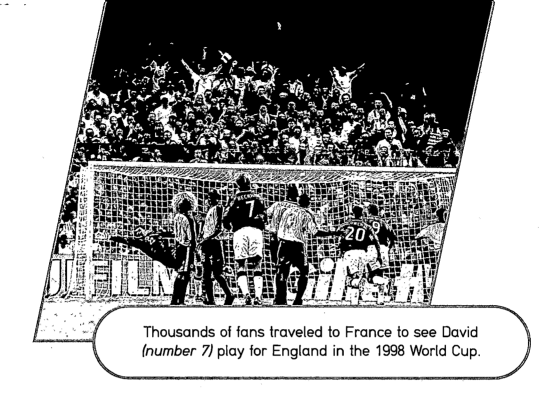

Thousands of fans traveled to France to see David
(*number 7*) play for England in the 1998 World Cup.

OVERCOMING DISASTER

Every four years, billions of soccer fans follow
the FIFA (Federation Internationale de Football
Association) World Cup. Teams from 32
countries compete in the monthlong World
Cup finals tournament. National pride is at
stake. Fans are desperate to see their national
teams do well. Players feel a ton of pressure.

In 1998, David was a member of England's team. He was just 23. His manager wasn't sure David could handle the pressure. But England was struggling. David was just too good to keep on the bench. His brilliant passing and a great free kick helped England win two key games. David became a national hero.

David *(left)* poses with England team manager Glenn Hoddle in 1998.

Then disaster struck! David lost his cool in a close game against Argentina. With the match tied 2–2, Argentine player Diego Simeone knocked David to the ground. David was furious. He reacted by kicking at Simeone.

The referee saw David's kick and gave him a **red card**. David was "sent off"—thrown out of

David *(right)* looks at the referee after Argentina's Diego Simeone knocks him down. David expected Simeone to get the penalty.

David *(left)* looks on in disbelief as the referee shows the red card.

the game. Worse yet, England had to finish the match one man short. They ended up losing. Millions of fans blamed David. Newspaper headlines called him "stupid," "idiot," and other insults. He even received death threats. No one felt worse than David.

The booing didn't stop when the 1998–1999 Man U season started. "It was hard concentrating," David admitted. But after a while, the booing just made him play harder.

David helped lead Man U to a historic season. His superb crossing passes produced many goals. "He is the best passer of a ball in the world," said star Ryan Giggs.

Man U became the first English team to win all three titles—the Premier League, FA Cup, and European Cup—in the same season! David's play had won over the fans again.

David and teammate Teddy Sheringham *(right)* celebrate winning the 1999 European Cup.

He had also won over Posh Spice. On July 4, 1999, David and Victoria were married at a castle. "Posh and Becks" moved into a big mansion. News photographers and TV cameras followed them everywhere. English soccer fans wanted to be just like David. When he changed his hairstyle, thousands of fans did the same.

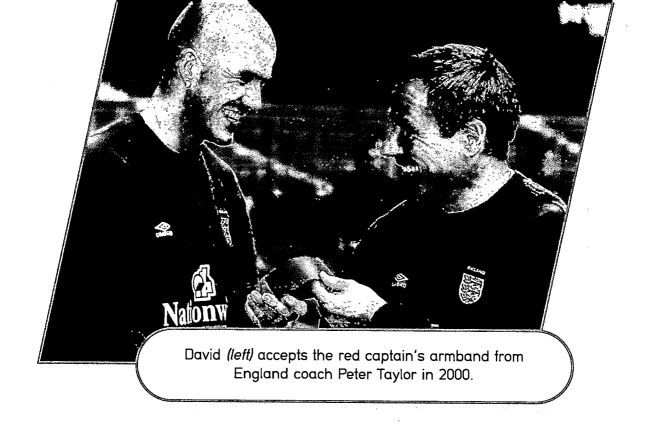

David *(left)* accepts the red captain's armband from England coach Peter Taylor in 2000.

NEW CHALLENGES

By 2002, David was on top of the world. He had helped Man U win four Premier League titles in five years. He was captain (team leader) of both Man U and England's World Cup team. He signed a new contract with Man U that made him the highest-paid soccer player in the world.

English fans had huge hopes for the 2002 World Cup finals. But a broken left foot slowed David. Still, he helped his team win a game on a penalty kick. He also set up two goals with perfect passes to win another match. But top-rated Brazil dashed England's World Cup hopes with a hard-fought win.

Meanwhile, Man U coach Alex Ferguson thought David's fame was getting out of hand. Ferguson wanted his team to focus on soccer, not superstars. So Man U sent David to the Spanish club Real Madrid for $41 million.

David *(right)* battles a Real Madrid teammate during a 2003 practice.

David *(left)* holds off a team Paraguay defender during the 2006 World Cup finals.

David was excited to have a new challenge. For the next four years, he dazzled fans with his magical passing and shot making. He led La Liga (the Spanish league) in **assists** in 2006.

During those years, David remained captain of England's national team for the 2006 World Cup finals. Once again, the hopes of a nation rested on his right foot. His goal against Ecuador made him the first English player to score in three finals tournaments. But England's World Cup dream ended when they lost to Portugal.

A few months later, rumors began to spread around the world. David Beckham was thinking about playing in the United States. American fans weren't sure what to make of it. The most famous soccer player in the world playing in the MLS? It all seemed too good to be true.

Yet the dream of millions of American soccer fans came true. In January 2007, soccer's greatest superstar announced he would join the LA Galaxy. He said playing for the Galaxy was another "new challenge." David, Victoria, and their three children moved into a mansion in Beverly Hills, California.

David (center) shows off his new Los Angeles Galaxy jersey.

David says, "I'm quite good at taking free kicks, but I practice them all the time. You need to practice to strengthen your weaknesses and maintain your strengths."

In the United States, soccer may never be as popular as football, baseball, and basketball. But David has already given the sport a huge boost. Millions of people who don't follow soccer have been tuning in to watch him play. Whatever happens, professional soccer in the United States will never be the same.

For David, it's all about sharing the sport he loves. "The buzz I get from playing football remains the same as it was when I was a kid growing up," said David, who never dreamed of being famous. "All I ever wanted to do was kick a football about."

Selected Career Highlights

2007   Joined Major League Soccer as member of Los Angeles Galaxy
Led Real Madrid to Spanish league title

2006   Became first English player in World Cup history to
score a goal in three World Cup tournaments
Led Spanish League in assists

2003   Joined Real Madrid team

2002   Scored winning goal to defeat Argentina in
World Cup match

2001   Runner-up for FIFA World Player of the Year
Scored tying goal versus Greece to qualify
England for World Cup
Led Manchester United to FA Premier
League Championship

2000   Led Manchester United to FA Premier League Championship

1999   Runner-up for FIFA World Player of the Year
Runner-up for European Footballer of the Year
Led Manchester United to European Cup title
Led Manchester United to English FA Cup title
Led Manchester United to FA Premier League Championship

1998   Led England to qualifying win for World Cup

1997   Named Professional Footballers' Association Young Player of
the Year
Led Manchester United to FA Premier League Championship

1996   Led Manchester United to English FA Cup title
Led Manchester United to FA Premier League Championship

Glossary

assists: passes to teammates that help score goals

contract: an agreement signed between a player and a team

corner kick: a direct free kick taken from the corner area after the ball is played out of bounds past the goal line by the defending team

crossing pass: a pass from one side of the field to the other

defenders: players whose job it is to try to stop the other team from scoring

English Premier League (EPL): the top league of English soccer teams. The team with the best record in Premier League play wins the Premier League title

European Cup: a yearly tournament held to decide the best team in Europe. Officially known as the Union of European Football Associations (UEFA) Champions League.

FA Cup: a yearly tournament in which professional English soccer teams compete to decide the country's top team. Officially called the Football Association Challenge Cup.

free kicks: special kicks awarded to teams when opponents commit penalties

midfielder: a position on a soccer team whose main responsibility is covering the middle of the field

possessions: plays when a player or a team has control of the ball

red card: a card given out by a referee for unsportsmanlike conduct. A player who is given a red card is sent off from the game, and the team must finish the game one player short.

trainee: a new player who learns the team's rules and plays

Further Reading & Websites

Pendleton, Ken. *David Beckham*. Minneapolis: Twenty-First Century Books, 2007.

Robinson, Tom. *David Beckham: Soccer's Superstar*. Berkeley Heights, NJ: Enslow Publishers, 2008.

Savage, Jeff. *Freddy Adu*. Minneapolis: Lerner Publications Company, 2006.

Wheeler, Jill C. *David Beckham*. Edina, MN: Abdo Publishing Group, 2007.

Los Angeles Galaxy: The Official Site
http://la.galaxy.mlsnet.com
The official website of the Los Angeles Galaxy includes the team schedule and game results, late-breaking news, biographies of David Beckham, and much more.

Manchester United: The Official Site
http://www.manutd.com
Manchester United's official website features news and game schedules, video highlights, player profiles, and history.

Sports Illustrated for Kids
http://www.sikids.com
The *Sports Illustrated for Kids* website covers all sports, including soccer.

Index

Photo Acknowledgments

Photographs are used with the permission of: AP Photo/Kevork Djansezian, pp. 4, 27; AP Photo/Mark J. Terrill, pp. 6, 7; © Stephen Dunn/Getty Images, p. 8; © Mike Egerton/EMPICS Sport/PA Photos, p. 9; © Mike Brett/PA Photos, p. 11; © Laurence Griffiths/EMPICS Sport/PA Photos, p. 13; © Michael Cooper/Getty Images, p. 15; © Chris Sunderland/Stringer/Reuters/CORBIS, p. 16; © POPPERFOTO/Alamy, pp. 18, 21; © Adam Butler/PA Archive/PA Photos, p. 19; © Gerald Cerles/AFP/Getty Images, p. 20; © Glyn Kirk/Action Plus/Icon SMI, p. 22; © Owen Humphreys/PA Archive/PA Photos, p. 24; © Liu Jin/AFP/Getty Images, p. 25; © Ross Kinnaird/Getty Images, p. 26; AP Photo/Pablo Martinez Monsivais, p. 29.

Front Cover: AP Photo/Mark Avery